JOY LAUREY

The Girl Who Pulled The Strings

The story of Joy Laurey and Mr Turnip

By Stuart Woodhead

Copyright © 2021

All rights reserved

Printed in the UK

First printed 2021

ISBN: 9798750566815

Edited by Louise Roberts

Cover by Daniel Hanton – Illustrator, Designer, Punch and Judy Performer.

For more related content, visit:

Our website - www.mrturnip.co.uk

Facebook - @thejoylaureyarchive

Twitter - @lawkylawkylum

Instagram - @thejoylaureyarchive

Or contact us at info@joylaurey.com

The Joy Laurey Archive

Dedicated to my mum Janine and dad Martyn for their unconditional love and for the amazing childhood they gave me.

Also, my partner Matt. I would not have been able to pursue my passions without his devotion and support.

Thank you.

CONTENTS

1. The Early Years — 1
2. The Laurey Puppet Company — 4
3. Snippet — 13
4. Mr Turnip and Whirligig — 19
5. Merchandise — 31
6. Puppets — 39
7. Shows and Performances — 42
8. Mickey Mouse Weekly and Cartoon Strips — 54
9. Gerry Anderson — 58
10. The First International Festival of Puppet Theatres — 64
11. Paul and Peta Page — 74
12. Retirement and Legacy — 77

CHAPTER 1 - THE EARLY YEARS

In the Restoration period, under the reign of King Charles II, the legendary puppet duo Punch and Judy made their debut. It was on this day – May 9th, 1662 – that the history of puppeteering begins and is carried, as you will see, by much of Joy Laurey's own lineage.

Joseph Grimaldi was an English actor, comedian and dancer who became the most popular entertainer of the Regency era. Working in theatres on Drury Lane and in Covent Garden, he was famous for his clown character 'Joey'. Visually striking for the time, his character make-up was detailed: starting with a white base colour for his face, neck, and chest, before adding red triangles on the cheeks, thick eyebrows, and large red lips set in a mischievous grin. Grimaldi's make-up has been widely used as a template by many clowns and entertainers to the present day.

Figure 1 - Grimaldi

An expert Punch and Judy Puppeteer (and rumoured famous Drury Lane clown) Samuel Laurey Augustus McCullock was Joy's great grandfather. It is believed that Samuel was the inspiration for a variety of The Laurey Puppet Company's most colourful characters and the foundation for the stage name 'Laurey'.

Joy Dorothy Johnson was born on April 30th 1924 in Southsea, Hampshire. She was the eldest daughter of Emily "Dorrie" (formerly McCulloch), a talented watercolour artist and performer who later became the president of The Royal British Legion. Joy was the older sister of Honor, who found her own fame in puppeteering under the stage name Peta Page, which will be discussed later. Her father, Sidney Johnson, started his Royal Navy career as a cadet at the age of 18. He trained aboard the HMS Ganges II, and later progressed to Communications Officer, serving in both World Wars. During the first World War, he saw action on over fifteen ships including HMS Victory I and II, HMS Dreadnaught and HMS Dolphin.

At around seven years old, Joy and her family moved from Sunk Island, near Hull, up the country to Flamborough Village, East Yorkshire, after her father was deployed to Flamborough Head Signal Station.

Both Joy and her sister Honor attended Flamborough Village School.

Figure 2 - Flamborough Head

One Easter Holiday, Dorrie found the perfect way to entertain her girls. Searching through magazines for craft ideas, she came across an article showing the readers how to make their own marionette. The trio set about crafting the puppet, and around three weeks later had created their very first clown. Excited to test out their new creation, Dorrie suggested they put a mirror against the wall to see what the puppet would look like as they shone a torch on it. Joy recollected the moment of "sheer magic" in a radio interview in 1997, the family struggling to believe their eyes as the clown seemed so real. This would be the start of the Laurey women's ongoing passion for puppets, and they would go on to create many more.

Joy and her sister continued their education at Bridlington High School for Girls, approximately four miles from their home. There they nurtured their love for puppetry, performing for their peers in a show held at Wesleyan Chapel, which was a huge success. When Joy was twelve, her father was transferred to another post, causing the family to leave the "wonderful place" of Flamborough.

CHAPTER 2 – THE LAUREY PUPPET COMPANY

In 1938, 'The Laurey Puppet Company' was founded. They often went by the name 'The Jonathan Laurey Marionette Company' despite there being no record of anyone named Jonathan Laurey existing. It is my belief that this male pseudonym was used to give the Laurey women a passage into show business. Using a pseudonym in an intrinsically male-dominated business was a typical approach for women hoping to circumvent the misogyny of the time.

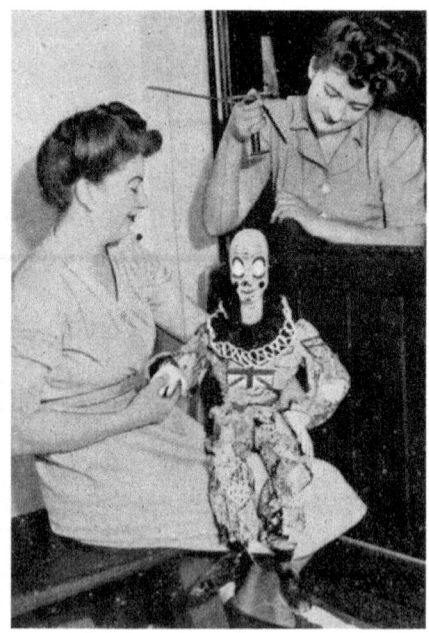

Figure 3 - Dorrie   *Figure 4 – Joy; Honour holding Patchwork*

Dorrie, her two daughters, and a rapidly growing cast were soon performing for people from all walks of life.

With the declaration of the second world war a year later, the male members of the expanded Laurey Puppet Company were drafted into His Majesty's Forces.

Dorrie wrote in *The Punch and Puppetry Pars*, April 1942:

> *"The women had picked up the work done by the male cast and hoped to launch puppets on definite war work."*

ENSA (Entertainment's National Service Association, affectionately known by troops as Every Night Something Awful) was established in 1939 by Basil Dean and Leslie Henson to provide entertainment for the British military. Many famous stars performed for ENSA, including Gracie Fields, Vera Lynn, George Formby, Tommy Cooper and Joyce Grenfell. During the war, ENSA performed over 2,650,000 times to over 300,000,000 servicemen worldwide.

Figure 5 - ENSA Logo

By October 1942, The Jonathan Laurey Puppet Company were performing "on the job" for ENSA. They travelled with nine puppets to entertain the troops, and were received with great interest and general acclaim everywhere they went.

During one memorable trip the family troupe got lost on their way to a performance and, entirely by chance, they happened upon an estate agent window where they saw a listing for their future home in Tiptree.

They gave shows to isolated units in difficult to reach and sometimes dangerous locations. This included Navy gun sites, dug-outs, Nissan Huts and forest clearings to troops awaiting battle. These were not stages, but War Zones!

To the troop's amazement they were given a sophisticated cabaret show. The people on the front row were asked to beam their torches on the puppets, bathing them in spotlight. Joy and her female entourage dressed for the occasion in long gowns, and there was even a female puppet who sat at a grand piano singing the Joyce Grenfell song 'There Is Nothing New To Tell You'. With the troops being away from their family and homes for extended periods, this lovely performance no doubt stirred emotions of bitter-sweet melancholy within the audience.

Joy and Honor gave a performance at South Baddesley Hall with all the proceeds going to 'The Wool Fund for Sailor Comforts'.

THE LAUREYS

BRITAIN'S ACE-GIRL PUPPETEERS

THE PUPPET STUDIO, TIPTREE, ESSEX   Tel. TIPTREE 133

Figure 6 – Honor (left) and Joy (right)

Ted Coney is a UK-based artist and lifelong fan of Joy's work. In research for an upcoming painting of his in the mid-1980s, he contacted Joy and, after much correspondence, they eventually met and a friendship was formed. In an article given to Ted by Joy called "Boat Show", Joy recollected a 'top secret' operation:

> *'It was an unusual day right from the start. My mother, my sister and I (Unit E39) were having a leisurely breakfast in our digs at Plympton, a small village just outside Plymouth, when our landlady brought us a letter which had been delivered by hand: our afternoon show had been cancelled, no reason given.*
>
> *It was unusual for us to ever have an afternoon off when we were on tour because we were entertaining mostly isolated units, gun sites, searchlight sites, RAF camps and so on, giving three shows a day. We decided to go to the cinema to see Dangerous Moonlight.*
>
> *We settled into our seats, looking forward to being entertained for a change, but barely 20 minutes into the first reel a hand-written notice was beamed onto the screen: 'Will ENSA Unit 39 please report to the manager's office immediately.'*

We tipped back our seats, scuttled out of the auditorium and went to find the manager. With him was a sailor, kitted out as a dispatch rider. After checking that we had all our props with us in the van, the manager told us to go with the naval dispatch rider. Baffled, we got into our van and followed him across Plymouth, through the dockyard gates to the side of a jetty.

At that moment an impressive naval launch slid quietly up to the jetty; the crew moored the boat, then the officer in charge saluted and, having checked who we were, asked us to come aboard. We explained that we had two large boxes full of puppets and a piano accordion. He arranged for these to be taken aboard and helped us down the slippery steps on to the launch. At this moment we caught sight of a disconsolate man in a German Officers uniform being quietly offloaded under heavy escort.

Once we were all clear of the jetty, the sub lieutenant said to us: 'Sorry about all this, but its top secret at the moment I'm taking you out to HMS Bulldog. We have just come back from freeing the Channel Islands and we can't give out any of our ship's company shore leave until the news has been released, so we thought an ENSA show would help the crew celebrate.'

Soon HMS Bulldog, at anchor, loomed into sight, and we had to clamber up a rope ladder slung over the ship's side – but we were more concerned that our boxes full of puppets might be emptied into the sea. In this event all was well, and we were ushered into the wardroom and invited to join the officers for dinner before the show.

What an occasion it was! Everyone was jubilant, and the captain explained that once they had completed their role as liberators, they were only too aware of the plight of the Channel Islanders. They had given them most of the food on the ship, and were very moved by their gratitude. A local schoolmaster had asked them if they could take some mail back to the mainland. Of course they said they would and during the next few hours it seemed that every person on the Islands had written to tell family and friends that their ordeal was over. Many bulging sacks of mail were delivered to the ship.

The Islanders said that they were embarrassed at having nothing to give their liberators in return, but a local fisherman came forward and presented the captain with two lobsters. These two lobsters were to become the high point of dinner that evening. With a flourish, the mess waiter served my mother, my sister, myself and the captain with half a lobster each – while the rest of the company looked on enviously. After dinner the captain conducted us to the forward mess deck which had been hastily decorated with flags. Members of the ship's company were perched everywhere, and the show went splendidly. We started as usual with a cabaret act, with our puppets operated in full view. Then my sister sang, accompanied by me on the piano accordion. We then moved onto requests and everyone sang their way through popular songs, from The White Cliffs of Dover to Roll out the Barrel.

We were well into our stride when the radio operator called us all to silence. He turned up the volume to enable us all to hear the BBC 9 o'clock news describing the liberation of the Channel Islands and the part played by HMS Bulldog. As various events were mentioned members of the crew would point to particular sailors, calling the 'radio star'. What an evening!

Eventually the captain called for silence and then thanked us for coming out and giving them such a great show. The crew cheered us to the echo, and the National Anthem was announced. I have played this on countless occasions but I don't think I have ever heard it sung with more enthusiasm or conviction."

Once back at our digs we could hardly believe the events of the previous eight hours. It is not every day that you have a chance to be part of history."

One of the showman's cases containing the puppets that Joy mentions is now a proud part of The Joy Laurey Archive.

Figure 7 - Showman's case

The officer they witnessed being escorted from the launch could well have been German Captain Lieutenant Zimmerman, who was captured after signing the Nazi surrender of the Channel Islands.

HMS Bulldog's most notable actions were the capture of a complete Enigma machine and codebooks from the German submarine U-110 in 1941, as well as sinking another German submarine in 1944. The surrender of the German garrisons of the Channel Islands was signed aboard the ship on May 9th 1945. Redundant after the war, she was broken up for scrap in 1946.

Figure 8 - HMS Bulldog

The Laurey Puppet Company travelled over 75,000 miles with ENSA.

When the war ended in 1945 and the company's work with ENSA was complete, Joy, Honor, and the rest of the company travelled back home. Once again, they could return to entertaining the British people in towns and seaside resorts across the country. This also gave Joy time to concentrate her skills on marionette making.

Dorrie strongly believed that puppets had a place in British Theatre, and in 1948 the company manipulated puppets for *Britannia Mews*, a film starring Maureen O'Hara (also known as *The Forbidden Street*).

Figure 9 - Stills from Britannia Mews

For many years, the company provided exclusive shows for the invitation-only 'Lord Mayor's Children's Party' hosted at The Mansion House, London. Once a year, the Lord Mayor would open The Mansion House, his home at the time, to the public. With fun to be had all around, the event typically featured (amongst other entertainments) a party and a fancy-dress competition.

In 1947, the Laureys entertained some 600 young guests at the Lord Mayor's Party where children were announced upon entry by footmen in powdered wigs! Performing in The Long Parlour, Dorrie said:

> *"It was certainly an occasion of great splendour. They had built a special platform for us in The Long Parlour on which we erected our own stage, and we presented "A Christmas Fantasia" in eight scenes. Our frontage is in*

white and gold, surrounded by black velvet drapes, and this merged most excellently into the existing scheme of decoration. Some 600 children all in fancy dress, all the dignitaries in their splendid robes of office, the crystal chandeliers, the elaborate upholstery, all gave one the impression of straying into the last act of "Cinderella".

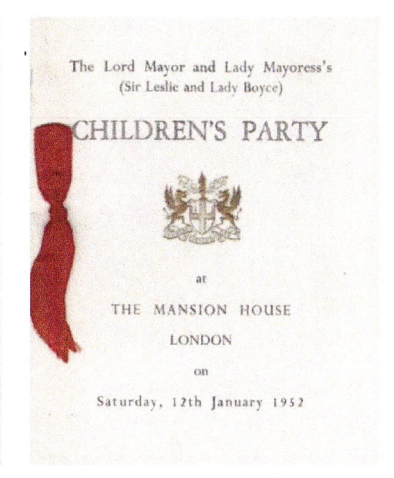

Figure 10 - Children's Party Invite (1947)

Figure 11 - Children's Party Invite (1952)

The Laurey Puppet Company had a busy schedule and would normally perform four or five shows during the day. As well as *A Christmas Fantasia*, they also performed *The Adventures of Snippet*, *The Jolly Swagman* and *The Syncopated Scarecrow*.

Joy and the company had a twelve-week season of puppet shows in 1949, performing *Summer Theatre* in Broadstairs, Kent. This charming old Georgian hall was situated just across the road from the house where Charles Dickens wrote *Barnaby Rudge*.

Figure 12 - Guest children in fancy dress with Snippet

CHAPTER 3 – SNIPPET

Before Mr Turnip, there was Snippet. In the form of a young boy, Joy created Snippet, and he became her first lead puppet and star of ensuing shows and books. He went on to give guest appearances, captivating the nation with his performances.

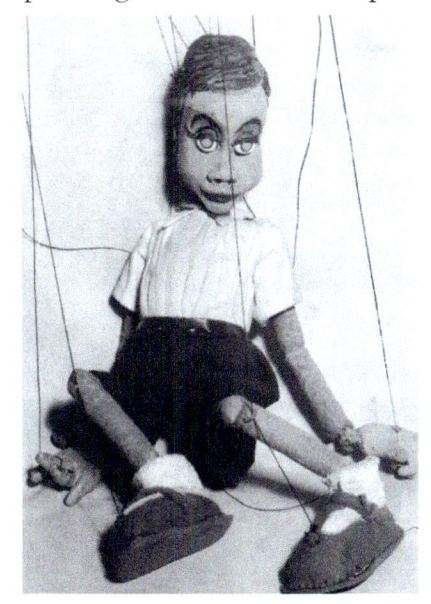

Figure 13 - Snippet

Figure 14 - Display board hand-painted by Joy

Figure 15 - Joy and Snippet performing on camera for BBC's 'Leisure and Pleasure'

Snippet was regularly featured on the cover of Enid Blyton's 'Playways' magazine. Enid Blyton was an English children's writer whose books have been among the world's best-sellers since the 1930s, selling more than 600 million copies. Her books are still enormously popular, and she is best remembered for creating 'Noddy', 'The Famous Five' and 'The Secret Seven' series. Snippet's presence in the work of this renown author is a testament to his popularity, despite being a lesser remembered creation of Joy's.

Figure 16 - Various 'Playways' edition covers, featuring "Fun with Snippet the Puppet"

Now an established studio in Broadstairs, the Laurey company could perform a variety of shows and plays for all ages, in which Snippet would make regular guest star appearances. There were even children's painting competitions with Snippet as the host.

Figure 17 - A poster for one of Snippet's painting competitions

Figure 18 - A girl playing with Snippet in Bognor Regis

Whilst performing one day, this little puppet captured the attention of BBC Producer Michael Westmore. He asked Joy if Snippet could be used for a new TV magazine programme called "Whirligig". The concept for *Whirligig* ended up changing drastically from its conceptual stage, casting a different presenter in need of an older puppet to accompany him. This resulted in the lively young Snippet being side-lined in favour of a more "Jiminy Cricket-esque" figure. Michael Westmore drew a rough image on the back of an envelope, exclaiming "Something like this, a Turnip!" and Joy was given just under a month to create one of the most complicated puppets of her career.

From Joy's imagination grew Mr Turnip, marking the start of a lifelong friendship!

Figure 19 - One of Joy's colour drawings of Mr Turnip

Figure 20 – Drawing references of Mr Turnip's head at different angles

Snippet remained a huge success and starred in shows with Joy for many years to come. Capitalising on the popularity of fellow puppet-star Mr Turnip, Joy also featured on BBC's *For Women: Leisure and Pleasure*, where she gave parents some hints and tips on handling string and glove puppets, accompanied by her beloved Snippet.

With the offer of a television contract already on the table, another opportunity came in for The Laurey Puppet Company to tour Australia! Joy was happy to start her TV career, whereas Honor, who was soon to marry fiancé Ian Robertson, thought they could use the cruise to Australia as their honeymoon. Honor and Ian would later become recognised puppeteers under the stage names of Paul and Peta Page.

With Honor and Ian away travelling, Joy and Dorrie hired some additional help, with Ann Davis joining as one of the new cast members. Davis attended art school and had been working as a theatrical costumier under director and designer Alec Shanks. With Davis's expertise in costume design, she was tasked with the creation of many stage outfits for the Laurey puppets over the next few years, both at York Gate Hall and for travelling to other venues.

Figure 21 - Snippet's tussle with a typewriter

After leaving The Laurey Puppet Company, Davis went on to create puppets of her own. One, Amanda the Cat, catapulted her to fame in Australia. Amanda was as famous to the Australians as Sooty and Basil Brush were to the United Kingdom. Davis successfully emigrated to Australia and built a very celebrated career, and I imagine Joy would have been very proud of her colleague and friend.

With stardom around the corner and Mr Turnip's replacement of Snippet, it's nice to think that Snippet would continue to remain with

Joy. After all, it was because of this little cheeky puppet that Joy was recognised for her work, catapulting her career and getting her name in lights.

I do often wonder how things would have gone if Snippet had continued onto *Whirligig* and not Mr Turnip, taking the place of everyone's favourite and treasured vegetable!

CHAPTER 4 – MR TURNIP AND WHIRLIGIG

When the BBC Television Studios moved to Lime Grove in Shepherd's Bush, it opened up the prospect of a live magazine programme for children, and *Whirligig* was born.

Mr Turnip made his live TV debut on November 25th 1950. His show aired biweekly on Saturdays at 5pm, alternating with *Saturday Special* hosted by Peter Butterworth and his parrot puppet Porterhouse (also voiced by Peter Hawkins). *Saturday Special* introduced many now-well-known names, such as Harry Corbett with Sooty and Tony Hart.

Many of the cast were fresh out of the military and had seen action in World War II.

Figure 22 - Michael Westmore and Mr Turnip

It was presented by Humphrey Lestocq (a former fighter pilot), affectionately known to everyone watching at home as HL. HL would habitually ramble and go off topic, and it was the job of Mr Turnip, voiced by Peter Hawkins, to keep HL on track. Peter Hawkins would later go on to provide voice overs for other shows such as *Bill and Ben the Flowerpot Men*, Blue Peter's *Bleep and Booster*, *SuperTed* and many more. Most notably, he provided voices for the hit sci-fi series *Doctor Who* as Daleks and Cybermen in the programme's early years.

Joy met the rest of the cast in a local pub. During the first rehearsal, Peter played around with several voices, and they all loved the one that would become the voice of Mr Turnip. In interviews, Joy would fondly recollect that all the cast and crew just happened to be the right people at the right time, and how it all came together in a very exciting way.

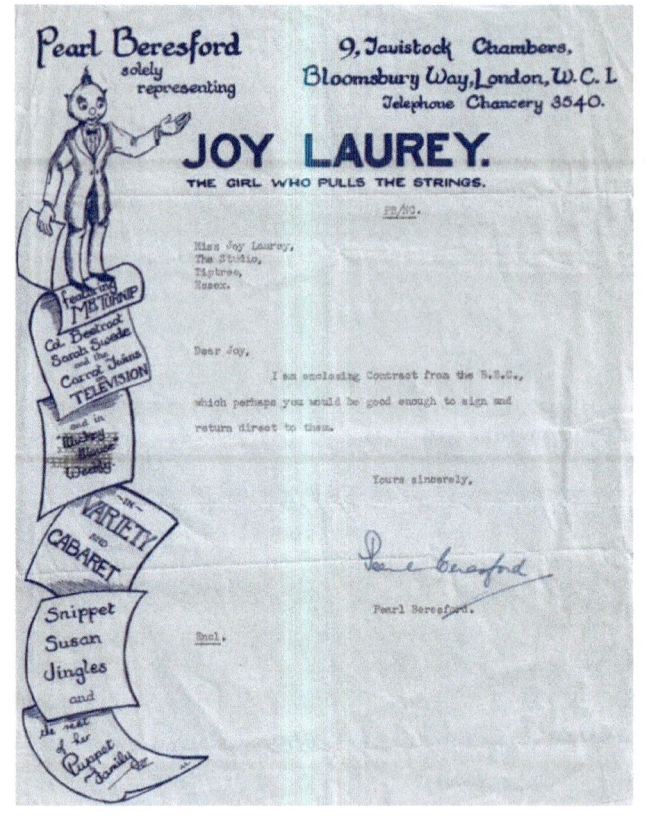

Figure 23 - Letter head

Mr Turnip was approximately twenty-one inches tall, and to ensure he could keep eye contact with HL, he was made with moving eyes. This was an important detail in giving him a lifelike quality, which was often used for comic and dramatic effect. To execute this movement, Joy used strings attached to the back of the puppet's eyeballs, enabling them to be manipulated separately. Joy referred to this as "serial stringing". With strings running through the interior of the body, a more subtle method of puppeteering was found, unlike the movement of Muffin the Mule which appeared more rigid in comparison.

Joy also added lead weights to the bottom of Mr Turnip's feet to prevent him from swinging after each movement. Being on live TV meant Mr Turnip needed to be more animated, resulting in more strings than a conventional puppet – twenty, to be precise, and a larger control bar.

Figure 24 - Behind the scenes photo of Joy as she manipulates Mr Turnip

Figure 25 - Mr Turnip and HL

Both Mr Turnip and HL had their own unique catchphrases, Mr Turnip's being "Lawky, Lawky, Lum" and HL saying "Goody, Goody Gumdrops".

HL and Mr Turnip were a dynamic duo. During filming, HL only ever concentrated on interacting with Mr Turnip, never paying attention to the puppeteers. He treated Mr Turnip like a real person. Joy always said that this "is why the pair worked so well together – they had chemistry".

Figure 26 - The chemistry between HL and Mr Turnip is tangible

In an unpublished story held by The Joy Laurey Archive, written by Peter Ling, Mr Turnip introduces himself:

> *"As we may not have met before, I think I had better start by telling you my name. I am Mr. Turnip. My birthday is on the eve of Halloween, but I can't tell you how old I am... It's either three hundred and something or four hundred and something – I can never remember the details. I wear a brown velvet coat, and smart green trousers, and my shirt has lace ruffles down the front. And of course I never go anywhere without my brief-case (which has my name on the side) and my umbrella."*

MR. TURNIP
B.B.C. TELEVISION STUDIOS
LIME GROVE, LONDON W.12

Figure 27 - Mr Turnip's calling card

In an interview many years later with Rowena White and Christine Glanville, Joy recalled:

> *"Of course, it was a live magazine programme and Mr Turnip provided the link between different items. I was marooned in the middle of the studio. It usually involved changing a puppet's costume during the show. This was no easy thing at the best of times and if a string broke there was no possibility of mending it. There was no way anybody could get to me during the show. It was an hour of breath-holding. Occasionally, I did have someone to help me, but by and large I was on my own. It was awesome as they would say nowadays, and really did sort out the men from the boys!"*

Over the years, many TV personalities made their debut on the show. *Whirligig* featured magician Geoffrey Robinson, Steve Race on piano, Harry Corbett with hand puppet Sooty, and Francis Coudrill's Hank the Cowboy. Within the main series, audiences could enjoy individual serials featuring Mr Turnip's adventures, such as 'Stranger from Space', 'Big Top' and 'Lost Property'. He was often joined by his vegetable friends Sarah Swede, Colonel Beetroot, the trouble Carrot Twins, and Mimi Melon.

Figure 28 - Mr Turnip   *Figure 29 - Mr Turnip with umbrella and case*

Col. Beetroot, runner-up for the Newman Cup, Takes Tea in Mr. Turnip's Garden.
by the Laurey Puppet Company.

Figure 30 - Exhibition image of a puppet tea party

Figure 31 - The Carrot Twins

Figure 32 - Sarah Swede

Figure 33 - Colonel Beetroot

Figure 34 – Mimi Melon

Children loved Mr Turnip, often sending him fan letters and presents in the post as if he was a real person. Tea cosies, chairs, cushions, a pipe and real tobacco, even furniture was received according to Joy, and they would often be placed on the house set ready for the filming of the next episode.

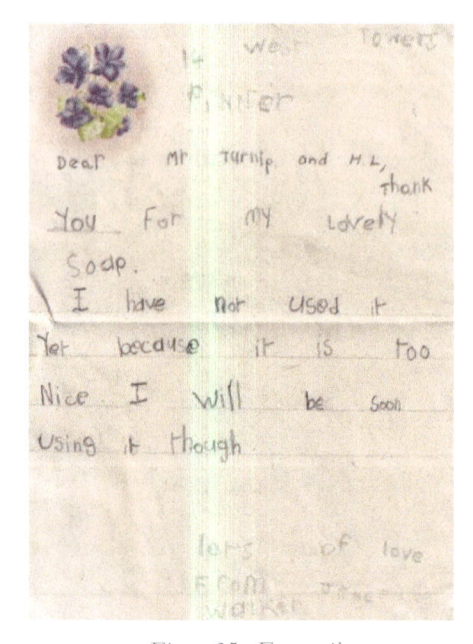

Figure 35 - Fan mail

Figure 36 - Mr Turnip in his onscreen home

Mr Turnip was appropriately dressed for any occasion, and Joy, along with her assistant Ann Davis, had the task of creating his ever-growing wardrobe. They ensured he was always perfectly attired and ready, whether he be piloting a plane or masquerading as a pirate.

Figure 37 - Set designer Richard Henry (left) with floor manager Bob Tronson (right) at the set of Mr Turnip's home

27

Whirligig was written by Peter Ling who went on to write many other well-known shows like *The Avengers, Doctor Who* and *Crossroads*.

The show ran from 1950 to 1956. Young TV fans were furious when the show announced it would be taking a break, protesting to the BBC and writing to The Mirror to complain.

Figure 38 - Joy with Mr Turnip on the telephone

Due to *Whirligig* being aired live, no recordings of the programme were made by the BBC. Small snippets of material recorded by fans at home have surfaced, however they are not widely available to the public. Sadly, none of the original episodes have survived as full recordings.

Much is the same for many other popular TV shows of the time: even if recordings were made, they are now missing or incomplete. The BBC were yet to realise the future potential of keeping archives of original recording footage, wiping their video reels to be reused due to their expensive nature. Good for profit and the spirit of recycling, not so good for television and pop culture history.

Doctor Who, now a massive franchise with an international and multi-generational appeal is another sad example, currently missing ninety-seven episodes. Even now, fans and collectors worldwide are constantly searching for them, and every so often a rare find is made!

In the absence of the original film reels, dedicated enthusiasts are making use of advances in technology to create their own interpretations of the missing footage. Starting with surviving materials such as production stills, tele-snaps and 'found audio' of the missing episodes recorded off-air by fans, these are cleverly combined with Computer Generated Imagery (CGI), digital animation or even Deep Fake Technology to run them together seamlessly.

We can only hope that one day an episode of *Whirligig* will be found. With the ever-widening age range of social media users, the power of popular video streaming websites and the growing trend of institutions making their archives available to the public digitally, it is perhaps only a matter of time.

Figure 39 - Behind the scenes photos of 'Whirligig' taken by Joy

Luckily in Joy's wide collection were some photo negatives. These are behind the scenes images of the show of various actors in Dutch costumes. I employed Henley Scan (photo and film restoration specialists) with the task of turning these into digital photos – this may be the first time these have seen the light of day!

Mr. Turnip was now a household name and popular celebrity in his own right, becoming the winner of the Daily Mail National Children's Television Award 1952-3. *Whirligig* also won programme of the year.

Figure 40 - Mr Turnip postcard

CHAPTER 5 - MERCHANDISE

As modern consumers, we are accustomed to the release of any new show bringing with it a tide of branded merchandise and endorsed products to maximise all potential profits. In the 1950s, however, such marketing methods were a new territory.

Being the puppet's creator, Joy found herself in the enviable position of being able to authorise various companies to produce Mr Turnip merchandise without needing permission from the BBC. Given the popularity of *Whirligig*, Joy naturally received an influx of offers for a variety of Mr Turnip related merchandise. She was happy to approve, and the flood gates opened!

Fans were soon able to buy branded board games, character soap, annuals, card games, pyjamas and even their very own Mr Turnip glove puppet.

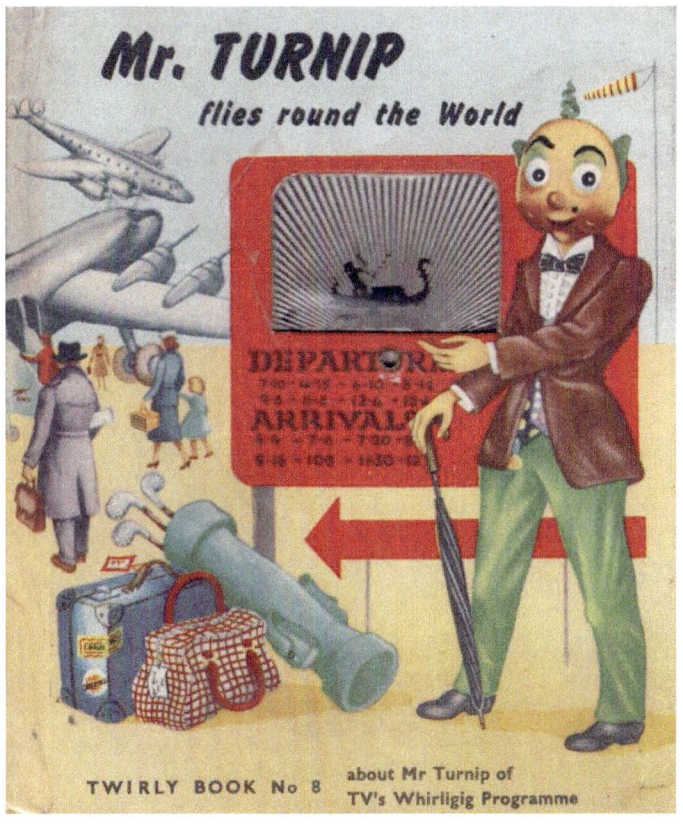

Figure 41 - Mr Turnip book 'Mr Turnip Flies Round the World'

Figure 42 - Mr Turnip soap

Figure 43 - Mr Turnip glove puppet

Figure 44 - Mr Turnip Painting Book 1

Figure 45 - Mr Turnip Painting Book 2

Figure 46 - Mr Turnip Goes Shopping

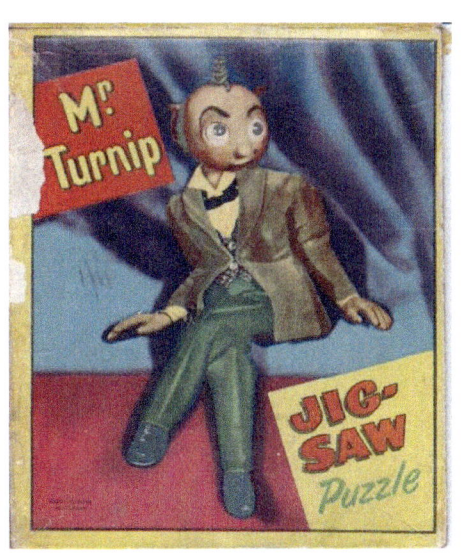

Figure 47 - Mr Turnip Jigsaw Puzzle

Adding even more to her workload, Joy dedicated herself to producing the artwork for the games featuring her puppet pal. Some fun examples are 'Mr Turnip's Bagatelle', a pinball game and 'Aerial Rings', all made by Glevum Games in the 1950s.

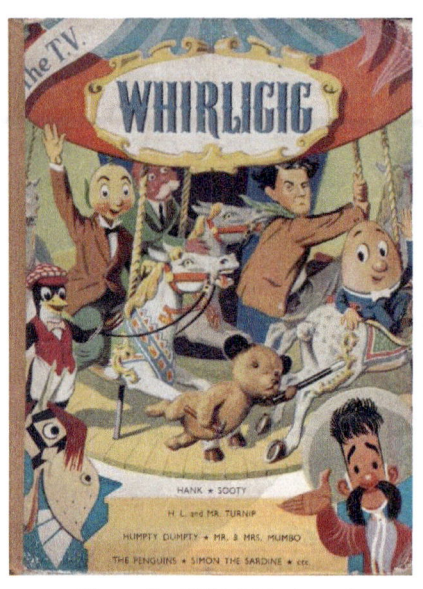

Figure 48 - 'Whirligig' Annual

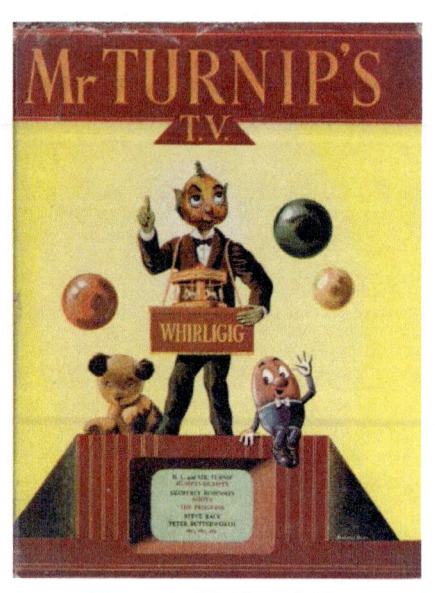

Figure 49 - Mr Turnip's TV

Figure 50 - Mr Turnip Bagatelle

Figure 51 - Mr Turnip's TV Audition card game

Figure 52 - Mr Turnip's Aerial Rings

Figure 53 - Lead Mr Turnip figurine by Luntoy

A News Bulletin at the time from Gordon and Gotch Ltd. Stated:

> *"Mr Turnip has indeed arrived. From now on he joins the honoured circle of Mickey Mouse and Horace Horsecollar. [...] It is a strange thought that up till recent times, England has had no national vegetable but from now on Mr. Turnip will stand for England as much as a leek stands for Wales and a Potato for Ireland."*

Figure 54 - Mr Turnip Pyjama fabric pattern

35

Pelham Puppets, a puppet-making company founded by Bob Pelham in 1946, were still in their early years when TV puppets started to gain popularity. Never one to miss out on an opportunity, Bob began recreating well-known TV characters reimagined as cleverly carved and snappily dressed hand-operated string puppets. They produced three amazing pieces under licence that matched the resemblance of Mr Turnip, Sarah Swede and Colonel Beetroot. Pelham Puppets boasted the individuality of each puppet due to their handmade nature. If you look closely, each puppet's head is produced from the same mould and adapted to each character.

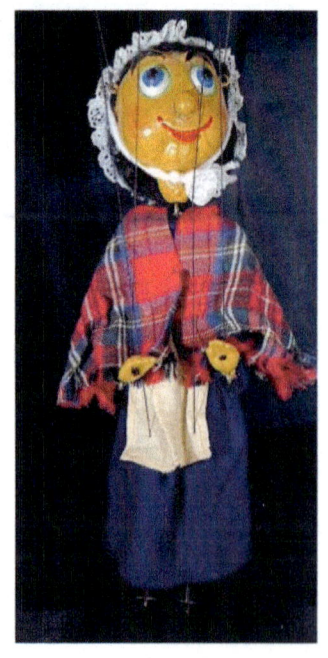

Figure 55 - Sarah Swede Pelham Puppet

Figure 56 – Colonel Beetroot Pelham Puppet

Pelham Puppets made a glove puppet version of Mr Turnip and went on to make other characters, such as Hank the Cowboy, Twizzle and many more Gerry Anderson favourites.

Members of the Pelham Puppets club, an international club of devoted puppet fans, were known as 'Pelpups'. In January 1952, a number of Pelpups were invited to a tea party held at the famous Harrods department store in London. There Joy, along with Mr Turnip, performed for one hundred lucky Pelpups!

Figure 57 - Mr Turnip Pelham Puppet

Figure 58 - Mr Turnip Pelham glove puppet

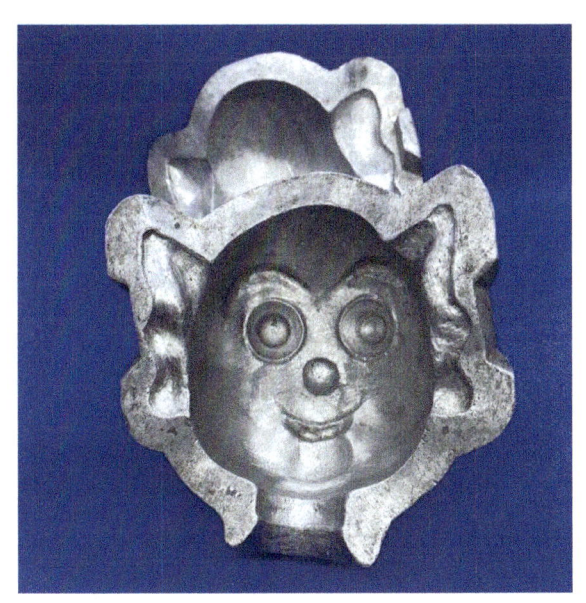

Figure 59 - The original Mr Turnip head mould from the Pelham Puppet factory

These children's toys are now very valuable and highly sought after by collectors and enthusiasts.

Figure 60 - Mr Turnip metal puppet

Joy certainly must have felt the pressure of Mr Turnip's growing merchandise endorsements, as well as working on the fortnightly *Whirligig* shows. Her daughter Julianna has said "She was such a fantastic mum […] we had a magical childhood because of her. We had all the Mr Turnip toys that all the other children wanted, and I've always remembered that."

The BBC, having seen the potential interest and subsequent revenue lost in their failure to fully license Mr Turnip, took precaution when licensing future material. Since *Whirligig*, all characters and shows belonging to the BBC have been fully licensed to ensure maximised profits, making Mr Turnip the vegetable that changed television history.

CHAPTER 6 - PUPPETS

Throughout her career Joy produced dozens upon dozens of puppets. Some, like Mr Turnip, became famous frontmen while others were what Joy referred to as "stock puppets," being reserved for more minor roles. In one episode these stock puppets may feature as a prince, the next recast as a member of a band, for example.

Joy made all of her own puppets by hand. A new project would take around six weeks and she would often work on up to three puppets at the same time. Crafting several characters simultaneously was more productive as this would allow Joy to work with the same crafting set-up, using the tools specific to one stage of the puppet-making process in one sitting, as opposed to putting them away and having to set them up again. Joy was also able to use her time more efficiently this way, switching between puppets as they were setting or drying. Some of her creations were made from papier-mâché whilst others were hand-carved, and The Joy Laurey Archive is fortunate to have string examples of both types in its collection. Joy also made glove and shadow puppets but is known best for her string puppets.

Many more may be hiding in other collections or waiting patiently in forgotten boxes to be found. We can only hope that the puppets of Colonel Beetroot, Sarah Swede and The Carrot Twins, all from *Whirligig*, will one day make an appearance. Snippet would certainly be a star again if he still exists.

Joy's sister Honor also made many puppets, but these were a larger more sophisticated type which will be explored in a later chapter.

Figure 61 - Patchwork

Figure 62 - South American singer

Figure 63 - Ebenezer Scrooge from 'A Christmas Carol'

Figure 64 - Abu Hassan from the play 'Abu Hassan'

Figure 65 - Omar from the play 'Abu Hassan'

Figure 66 - Caliph from the play 'Abu Hassan'

Figure 67 - A peasant gypsy woman

Figure 68 - Scarecrow

Figure 69 - Lucy, a South American singer

CHAPTER 7 - SHOWS AND PERFORMANCES

After the second world war, holidaying abroad became inaccessible to much of the British population. With extensive travel unaffordable for the average family, the classic seaside proved to be a popular alternative. City-dwellers flocked to the coast with their families, renting cottages and chalets or heading to holiday camps such as Butlins. Coastal destinations such as Blackpool, Scarborough, Brighton and Bognor Regis became popular places to go and provided a change of scenery, plenty of fresh air and fun for the whole family.

As a result, many performers also flocked to these seaside resorts to provide entertainment for the influx of holiday-goers. By regularly putting on showcases and hosting variety galas at these popular locations, performers were able to secure a steady income for themselves. Among many others, some of the more famous artists who benefited from this post-war prosperity included Percy Bee the magician, Harry Corbett with puppet Sooty, and Dave Cecil whose stage names included both Charles Cole the cartoonist and Windy Blow the famous balloon clown.

Figure 70 - Charles Cole's business card

Tabloids claimed there was a time that Dave Cecil couldn't blow out a match! After losing one lung in The Battle of Anzio in 1944, Cecil was given just one year to live. Whilst in the hospital, however, a doctor urged Cecil to "have a go" at blowing up some balloons, thinking it could help him gradually build some lung strength. It took regular practice before he was able to blow up even a single balloon, but soon after there was no stopping him. Cecil was making swans, giraffes and other silly shapes, keeping his fellow patients entertained and making them laugh. His kindness was repaid when a man in a neighbouring bed gave him the formula to make his own balloons.

Dave Cecil decided that, if he lived, he would go on stage and perform balloon shows professionally, and so Windy Blow the Silent Tramp Clown was born. Windy Blow was a huge hit, and before long Cecil and his wife would start a small balloon factory in their garage in order to make enough balloons to keep up with the growing popularity of his act.

Figure 71 - Business card for Windy Blow

Windy Blow made his debut in 1953 and starred in the first ever *TV Music Hall* in 1954.

Windy only ever spoke once in his silent career. In 1955, an article from *Illustrated* reported that Windy was performing at a party for U.S. Servicemen and had given some balloon toys to a black girl in the audience. The girl took her prize back to her seat where some of the white children deliberately popped them.

Regarding the incident:

> *"Windy saw red! He'd never spoken before, but he said something then. He called that little girl back and made every toy he knew — specially for her. As she went back to her place a second time she handed nearly all of them to the white children!"*

Harry Corbett, Dave Cecil's contemporary, also made his career as an entertainer in post-war Britain. Corbett found the glove puppet who would be known to the world as Sooty in a joke shop, on Blackpool North Pier in 1948. This chance encounter would send Corbett to stardom as the pair became instantly popular following their appearance on BBC's *Talent Night*. Shortly afterwards the BBC gave Sooty his very own series, and while Harry and Sooty became famous on-screen characters, they also travelled to perform their act live.

Joy and Harry Corbett were both represented by the same agent; Pearl Beresford was a well-respected talent scout and manager of many popular entertainment acts. Joy and Corbett worked together at Family Fun Days for many years, and when Corbett retired, his son Matthew took over operating and starring alongside Sooty. The act had now grown to include fellow hand puppet friends Sweep the Dog and Soo the Panda.

Joy Laurey
THE LAUREY PUPPETS

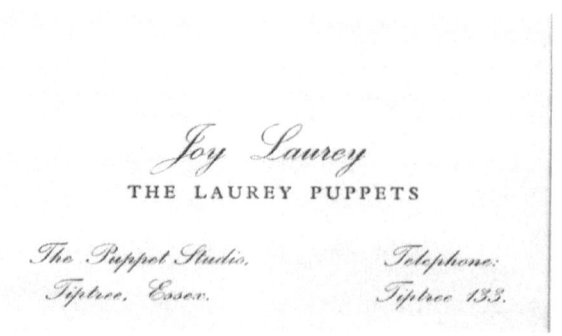

The Puppet Studio,   Telephone:
Tiptree, Essex.   Tiptree 133.

Figure 72 - Joy's business card

Sooty is currently in the hands of Richard Cadell, and together they have entered into the Guinness Book of Records for the longest-running children's TV programme in the world.

In the warmer months, Joy joined fellow performers at the seaside with her collection of puppets, which included Snippet and her now-famous TV personality puppet Mr Turnip. Joy cleverly used a crackly old recording of Peter Hawkins – the voice of Mr Turnip on *Whirligig* – at her shows.

Figure 73 - Joy and Mr Turnip entertaining at a party

Floral Hall, Scarborough, was built in 1911 with a capacity of 1500 seats and additional room for standing. Through the years it has hosted many recognisable names, including Lonnie Donegan, Les Dawson, The Krankies and the famous Fol de Rols. This renowned dancing troupe whose act included the use of choreographed puppets later performed with specially Pelham Puppets as well as, of course, Joy Laurey and Mr Turnip.

Figure 74 - Floral Hall poster 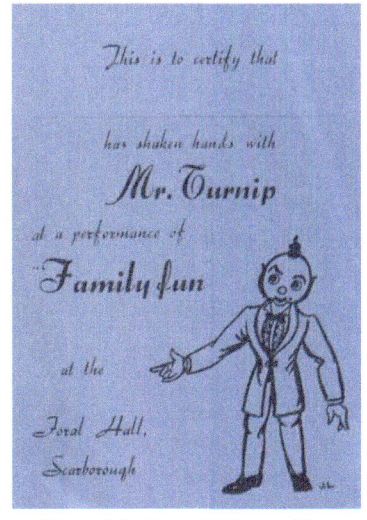 *Figure 75 - Participation certificate*

During her interview with Elaine Bamford for her book on Tiptree, Joy recalled that one show's crowning of King and Queen narrowly avoided catastrophe – the troupe discovered they had no crowns! Thinking on her feet and using her natural artistic ability, Joy offered to quickly make some crowns using nothing more than gold card and sugar pastels. I wonder how long the sugar pastels lasted on those crowns, or if they're still intact today?

Figure 76 - Joy with Mr Turnip, Percy Bee, Windy Blow the Clown with crowned party Queen, and Harry Corbett with Sooty

In conversations with friends, Joy often recalled travelling back and forth between Scarborough and Bridlington to perform various acts at different shows. The Mr Turnip puppet she used for seaside shows needed to be bigger than that used for TV so the audience in these larger venues could see him. She made a replica 1.5 times larger than the TV puppet, which she later confessed to burning – in her eyes there could only ever be one true Mr Turnip!

In the 1950s, Joy and the The Laurey Puppet Company began to let York Gate Hall in Broadstairs, Kent, during the holiday seasons. This Grade II listed building was originally built to house the armour collection belonging to Sir Guy Laking in 1911, and was later used by the council to store beach equipment. The company occupied it and turned it into a theatre. After their occupancy ended, York Gate Hall was transformed into a cinema. It is now called The Palace Cinema and remains the only cinema in Broadstairs.

Figure 77 - The Palace Cinema (2021)

With Cambridge University within easy travelling distance, The Laurey Puppet Company would often temporarily employ one or two undergraduates. This worked well for both parties as the students were available to work during the summer season when the puppet company was at its busiest. They often took turns to compere when Dorrie reportedly became ill. Notably Ian Robertson, one of the undergraduates, would go on to marry Honor.

The puppet troupe performed many shows during their time in Broadstairs, including *A Christmas Carol*, *The Tinder Box* and *The Entwhistles Entertain*.

Figure 78 - Postcard with still from 'The Tinder Box'

SCROOGE AND BOB CRACHITT
from the Laurey Puppet Production of "A Christmas Carol," by Charles Dickens

Figure 79 - Postcard with still from 'A Christmas Carol'

Sir Ralph Richardson was an actor who, alongside John Gielgud and Lawrence Olivier, was known as one of the trinity of male actors who dominated the British stage during the 20th century. Sir Richardson attended one of the productions at York Gate Hall, calling it "A Wonderful Show!". The Laurey company was delighted, and included the quote in the following year's programme.

When the Laureys were travelling home to Tiptree at the end of a successful summer season at Broadstairs, a Jeep ran out of control and crashed into their van. Driven by Honor, the van was flipped onto its side with such force that the body of the van was ripped from the chassis. Honor and husband-to-be Ian Robertson escaped unscathed, but the van's contents of show equipment was strewn over a large part of the road. Luckily nothing was irreparably damaged.

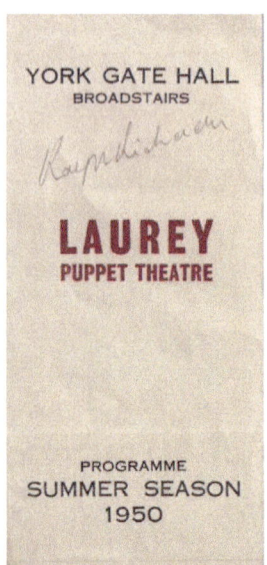

YORK GATE HALL
BROADSTAIRS

LAUREY
PUPPET THEATRE

PROGRAMME
SUMMER SEASON
1950

Figure 80 - Theatre programme signed by Sir Ralph Richardson

Figure 81 - York Gate Hall postcard

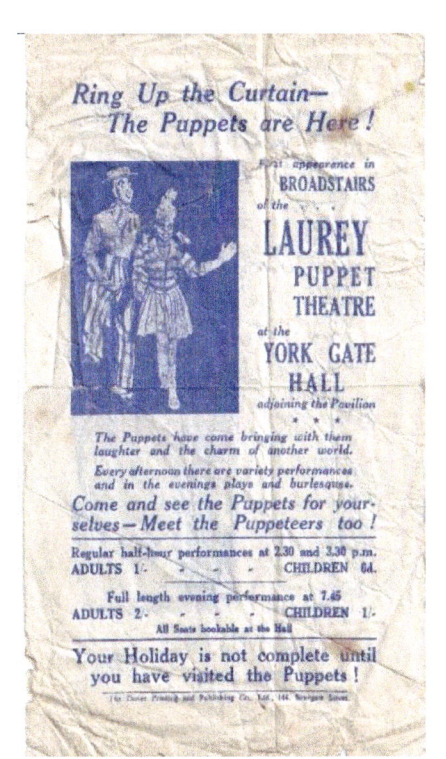

Figure 82 - A flyer from the first year in Broadstairs

Figure 83 - York Gate Hall poster

49

On September 24th 1952, *The East Kent Times* published the following article regarding the popularity of The Laurey Puppet Company's shows:

> *"The Laurey Puppets gave their last performance of the season to an appreciative audience in the York Gate Hall, Broadstairs, on Saturday.*
>
> *After the show, Councillor L. P Donne spoke of the pleasure the Laurey Puppets had brought to hundreds of visitors to Broadstairs - both grown-ups and children during the five seasons they had appeared there. "I feel sure" he said "that I speak for residents and visitors alike in wishing them a speedy return."*
>
> *Bouquets were presented to Dorrie Johnson, Joy Laurey and Ann Davis; and their assistants. David Robinson, Roger Pew and Nigel Drewe, were handed tokens of appreciation.*
>
> *Great interest was aroused by the novel presentation to Joy Laurey of a cake in the form of a television set, the screen of which showed a close-up of her popular television puppet, Mr. Turnip.*
>
> *Councillor Donne caused great amusement by demonstrating a new miniature harmonica before presenting it to Snippet, the irrepressible puppet favourite of visitors to the Laurey Puppet Theatre.*
>
> *Thanking Councillor Donne, Dorrie Johnson said "We greatly appreciate the way in which Broadstairs has taken us to its heart, and we are all looking forward to being back again next year."*

In 1953, the year of the Queen's Coronation, The Laurey Puppet Company created three new shows and a Coronation Masque. They held regular live shows and hosted many guest performers, most notably Annette Mills who hosted her own puppetry programme *Muffin the Mule,* which aired on alternating weeks to *Whirligig*. In her TV show, Annette talked to the audience at home and played the piano whilst string puppet Muffin danced along. Annette would relay Muffin's thoughts to the audience as he whispered into her ear. Muffin was made by the famous puppet maker Fred Tickner for Jan Bussell and Ann Hogarth.

In her appearance for The Laurey Puppet Company, Annette brought along her hand puppet Prudence the Kitten. Prudence's character was styled as Annette's faithful friend and housekeeper. She later featured in her own self-titled comic strips and books, including 'My Annette Mills Gift Book' where she can be seen accompanied by other of Mills' fictional characters such as Charlie Parkin and Colonel Crock.

Figure 84 - Annette Mills with Prudence at Broadstairs

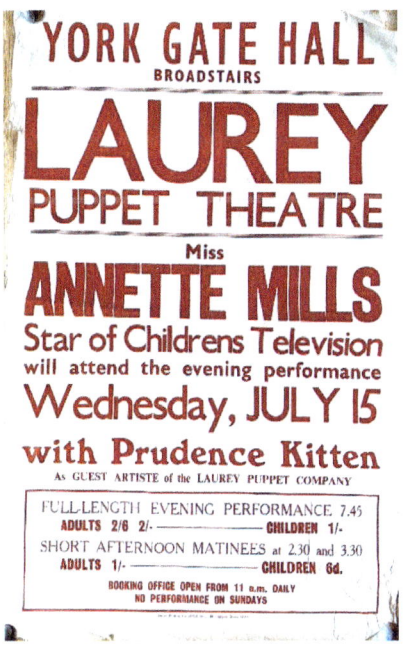

Figure 85 - Poster for Annette Mills at York Gate Hall

Despite mainly working behind the scenes at York Gate Hall, Joy was still well-known in the entertainment and media business, and several famous artists chose her as their subject.

Ralph Sallon worked for the Daily Mirror at the time, producing regular caricatures of contemporary figures. Sallon would often wait with press photographers outside London hotels, hoping to catch a look and draw a quick sketch of a celebrity before they disappeared.

Another famous name to capture Joy was Stirling Henry Nahum – more famously known as Baron. He took some amazing portrait photos of both Joy and Mr Turnip.

Figure 86 - Sallon's sketch of Joy and Mr Turnip

These photos, both signed by Baron, have to-date not even been seen by the National Portrait Gallery which holds nearly all of Baron's work.

Figure 87 - Joy puppet-making and sketching as she sits for Baron

A friend of the late Prince Phillip, Baron was appointed official court photographer. He had the privilege of photographing the Royal Wedding of the Queen and Prince Phillip, and was also the official photographer for the Queen's Coronation. Other celebrities who sat for Baron include Marilyn Monroe, James Stewart, Christopher Lee, Winston Churchill and Marlene Dietrich to name but a very small amount, so Joy must have surely felt like a star.

Lucy Dawson who used the pseudonym "Mac" also captured Joy in one of her paintings. She was, however, best known for her dog portraits and was famously commissioned a number of times to paint the prestigious Royal family Corgi, Dookie. Her illustrations are in numerous children's books and many British and American publications.

Figure 88 - Mac's painting of Joy and Mr Turnip

Figure 89 - A sketch of Joy done by Mac: "Can you lend a hand or pull a string?"

CHAPTER 8 - MICKEY MOUSE WEEKLY AND CARTOON STRIPS

Mickey Mouse Weekly was a Disney magazine published by Odhams Press that ran from 1936 to 1957.

The magazine contained comic strips featuring classic Disney characters such as Mickey Mouse, Donald Duck and Peter Pan, to name a few. It also showcased characters not belonging to Disney like Robin Hood and Davy Crockett, as well as stories from renowned children's authors such as the aforementioned Enid Blyton.

The *Mr Turnip Adventures* was one of the magazine's comic series and was very popular, running for numerous instalments. Eager to archive everything relating to her beloved Mr Turnip, Joy cut out and saved any mention of him and his growing fame that she could find from the press. There are over one hundred comic strips that Joy faithfully saved, and often duplicated, in her collection.

The team behind Mickey Mouse Weekly created a fan club called the Jungle Chums, and in 1951 they asked Joy if she would do a performance for the club members. Many attended this exciting event at York Gate Hall, enjoying the opportunity to see the amazing TV character Mr Turnip in person. Those who attended received a special rosette-style card gift tag they could proudly pin to their clothing, becoming the envy of their friends.

Figure 90 – The Jungle Club rosette

Figure 91 - Jungle Chums ready to enter York Gate Hall (1951)

Figure 92 - York Gate Hall (2021)

MICKEY MOUSE WEEKLY—September 1, 1951

HALLO, Jungle Chums, everywhere. This is Robin Alone speaking. Remember last week I told you to keep your eyes open for more exciting club activities? Well, this week I can tell you about our next outing. It's going to be a visit to see a special showing of Mr. Turnip, the famous Television Puppet.

Miss Joy Laurey and her Puppet Company are now at Broadstairs, Kent, where she is giving daily shows at the York Gate Theatre. Mr. Turnip is there, too, when he isn't at the B.B.C.'s television studios rehearsing and preparing for his next T.V. Whirligig programme.

Mr. Turnip's Idea

Miss Laurey tells me that Mr. Turnip suddenly thought it would be a good idea to give a special show for a hundred Jungle Chums. And at what better place could it be than a holiday resort? None so far as I know. So now Miss Laurey and Mr. Turnip are busily working out the details of the show, and in the meantime I have sent out invitations to Jungle Chums who live within a reasonable distance of the theatre.

There is no need for Chums to write in, for full instructions have been given to all those invited.

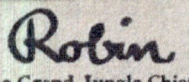

Robin
The Grand Jungle Chief
128 Long Acre, London, W.C.2.

Figure 93 - Jungle Chums article, featuring 'Mr Turnip's Idea' column (1951)

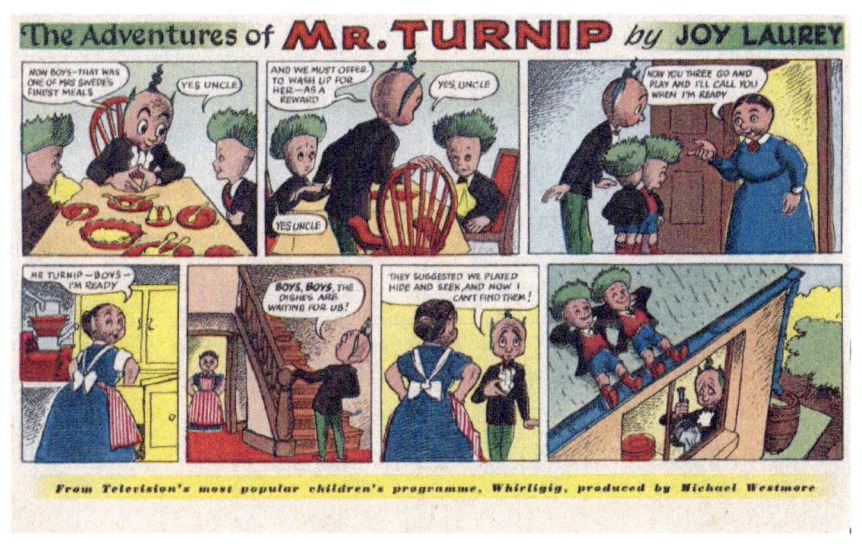

Figure 94 - 'The Adventures of Mr Turnip' strip: Hide and Seek Goes Wrong

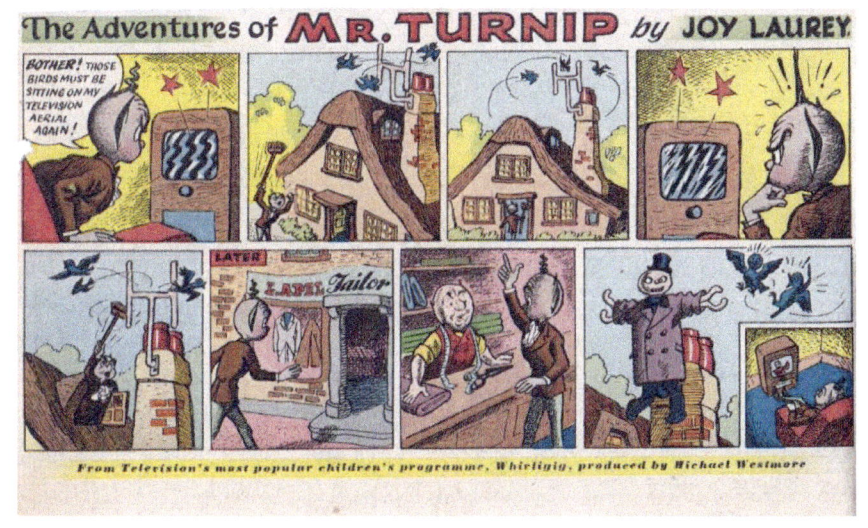

Figure 95 - 'The Adventures of Mr Turnip' strip: Mr Turnip Has an Idea

CHAPTER 9 - GERRY ANDERSON

1955 saw the creation of 'Independent Television' a new TV channel more commonly known as ITV. Based on the successful *Adventures of Noddy* book series by Enid Blyton, Independent Television created a new children's puppet-based programme to rival Muffin the Mule. As an indicator of the show's success, Noddy was licensed by Kellogg's for their cereal 'Sugar Ricicles', featuring him in their advertising campaign. The Sugar Ricicles TV commercial was made by Pentagon Films Ltd in 1956.

Figure 96 – Kellogg's advert featuring Noddy

Roberta Leigh, another children's author at the time, had recently secured a television commission for her book, *Twizzle,* about a toy with a unique talent. Twizzle was a doll with the ability to extend his arms and legs who had escaped from a toy shop to embark on adventures, meeting new friends along the way. Leigh now had the task of finding a production company to transform *Twizzle* into a children's program for Independent Television. Gerry Anderson, the co-director of Pentagon Films at the time, met with Leigh and, upon seeing the script, gave an enthusiastic "Yes!" to the author, only to find out with much disappointment that it would be made using puppets.

Around the same time, Gerry Anderson and Arthur Provis decided to set up A.P. Films (Anderson Provis Films) with the pair wanting to concentrate on film and TV productions instead of commercials. They left Pentagon Films but told Leigh they still wanted to produce *The Adventures of Twizzle* as it may be a lucrative way of making themselves known as a new name in the television industry.

In 1957 A.P. Films set about making fifty-two episodes of *The Adventures of Twizzle,* with a budget of £450 per fifteen minute episode.

Knowing very little about puppets, Gerry Anderson arranged to meet the well-known and respected TV puppeteer Joy Laurey, who her agent Pearl Beresford promoted as 'the girl who pulls the strings'. He had seen her work with famous children's TV character Mr Turnip on the BBC's *Whirligig.*

Following their meeting, Joy visited A.P. Films several more times. Along with a creative brief and some sketches, she made all the puppets for the show. Interestingly, Anderson's first wife, Betty Wrightman, made the puppet's clothes and sets herself.

In a letter to her friend and colleague Christine Glanville, dated August 16th 1957, Joy spoke about her upcoming work with A.P. Films:

> *"I too feel that this is a wonderful opportunity, and may well be the beginning of something big!"*

Roberta Leigh had commissioned a designer to draw defined-colour-images for Joy to work with, and Joy was given a mere three weeks to make her puppets ready for filming. She constructed them mainly from papier-mâché and, in the rush to complete them, Joy was concerned with Twizzle's awkward shape as it had left him unbalanced. However, upon meeting with Leigh, and receiving the author's approval on Twizzle's final design, Joy was left to her own devices with the other characters.

Islet Park Country Mansion – the beautiful, privately owned, Edwardian stately home in Maidenhead – was the base of operations for A.P. Films and provided accommodation for the crew. Despite the puppeteer's bridge being very basic (with some remarking that it resembled a Meccano structure) the glamorous Rococo-style ballroom was used for the set. In fact there wasn't much room for the puppeteers on the bridge at all: although the room was over twelve foot high with its ornate ceiling, there was only enough room for the puppeteers to crouch, and Joy recalled that the bridge often bowed in the middle when multiple people were on it.

The schedule was tough and those were long days. Tensions began to grow and Sylvia Thamm, who oversaw continuity (and later married Gerry Anderson), thought a break was needed. Being near to Christine Glanville's birthday, Joy decided to book a trip with her friend to see Judy Garland in London. Joy and Glanville enviously watched Judy Garland (now-famously) sit on the edge of the stage, flooded by spotlight and perform 'Over the Rainbow'. What an amazing and unforgettable experience.

Joy, Christine Glanville and The Laurey Puppet Company's Murray Clark operated the puppets for all fifty-two episodes recorded from September 1957 until December 1958, of which sadly only the first episode is known to have survived.

Figure 97 - Twizzle

The *Woman's Hour* radio programme aired a special feature on the bygone puppets of children's television in 1997. This episode mentioned puppets such as Otis the Aardvark, Andy Pandy, Little Weed, Huxley Hair and many more. Ever his champion, Joy was disappointed that the show failed to mention Mr Turnip, and called the show in hopes to correct their omission. This resulted in her being invited to discuss her lifelong passion for puppetry as a guest on the show, allowing Joy to talk in detail about some of her more famous characters, including Twizzle. She explained to radio interviewer Jo Morris that she in fact made two Twizzle puppets for the show: one with regular proportions that was suited for walking and dancing, and another with 'twizzling' telescopic arms and legs to show off the character's trademark trick. One of Twizzle's on-screen friends was Jiffy the Broom Stick Man who often gave Twizzle a ride as they flew off on an adventure, and Joy remembered him being great fun to make with his lacquered sticky-up hair.

When the TV series production came to an end in 1958, Joy decided to leave A. P. Films to concentrate on other projects and stage work. Her friend and assistant, Christine Glanville, stayed on with A.P. Films to work on their next puppet-based production *Torchy the Battery Boy*, also written by Roberta Leigh, which turned out even bigger and better.

Christine Glanville would continue to work with Gerry Anderson for over four decades. With her puppetry being expertly honed from working alongside Joy and receiving creative direction from Gerry Anderson, Christine became one of the industry's leading puppeteers. She went on to work on the 1986 cult classic film *Labyrinth* starring David Bowie and featuring iconic animatronic puppets by Jim Henson's 'Creature Shop', where she operated one of the goblins.

Figure 98 - Mistress Quercus (left) and Septimus (right)

Gerry Anderson went on to make globally successful shows like *Thunderbirds*, *Stingray*, *Captain Scarlet* and *Terrahawks*, each using a variety of different puppetry styles. He eventually made a move into live action shows, producing *UFO* and *Space 1999*.

As Gerry Anderson moved more and more towards the human form, Joy became disillusioned. Something recalled by Joy's friend Ted Coney from a conversation they had in her later life.

> *"Joy didn't feel puppets were meant to be like humans – she thought they were something completely different"*

In 1998, Joy had one final brush with TV puppetry when she devised her own show. Written by William Thatcher, *Septimus* was about a Gargoyle boy that came to life and could time travel. Despite the puppets being ready, scripts written and story boards drawn up, the BBC rejected the concept. Anglia TV expressed an interest, but despite promising its production, the show was unfortunately never produced or televised.

Figure 99 - Storyboard for 'Septimus', hand-drawn by Joy

STORY BOARD FOR SEPTIMUS.
(First episode).

1. Steeplejack arrives in his van, and prepares to scale the church face.

2. Shot of church face, showing the external sculptures and features on the church.

3. Close-up of Septimus looking like a stone image.

4. Wide angle shot of the view from the top of the church.

5. Jack (the steeplejack) reaches the top of the ladder, and starts cleaning the image of Septimus. This makes Septimus sneeze and come to life. Jack is shocked and amazed, and starts talking to himself.

6. Septimus starts to talk to Jack, but it is in "old English". They both chat and ask questions. Septimus introduces Jack to the other statues. Jack then eats his sandwiches and Septimus is amazed at the food he is eating (having been a statue for hundreds of years, he has never seen things like bananas etc).

7. Shot of two noble statues, who communicate with each other using sign language.

8. Shot of nosey gargoyle who makes gargling noises.

9. Shot of the weather-cock, who shouts out the weather in a squawk at the top of its voice.

10. A peep through a gap to see "Mistress Quercus" (oak), who is the chatelaine under the boards of the tower. She keeps all the church creatures in order.

11. Group of church mice who sing in Latin, also a spider. Quercus feeds them cheese to deter them from gnawing through the church woodwork.

12. Closing shot of Septimus who waves goodbye when its Jack´s home time.

© Joy Laurey   January 1998.

1

Figure 100 - Accompanying text for the storyboard

CHAPTER 10 - THE FIRST INTERNATIONAL FESTIVAL OF PUPPET THEATRES

Joy Laurey regularly travelled around the world to attend international puppet festivals. Taking her puppet creations with her, she would perform in-front of both visiting spectators and her peers – the very best puppeteers in the world!

Figure 101 - Programme from the festival's debut year

The very first International Festival of Puppet Theatres was held in Bucharest in 1958. Harry Siegel, the director of the Marionette Theatre in Braunschweig, called it "the giant of Bucharest". The festival featured thirty companies from fifteen countries, producing nearly one hundred performances across fifteen days. The festival was attended by over 35,000 spectators and puppeteers from five continents travelled to perform there. Showing a real diversity of styles, the festival showcased anything from big ensembles including tens of artists with decades of experience, to smaller troupes and even individuals with their puppets and personal belongings sharing the same travel trunks.

Joy performed with her beloved and now very famous Mr Turnip, representing both The Laurey Puppet Company and Great Britain.

The following was translated from the 1958 festival programme:

'Recital Joy Laurey

A NEW FIRST SUMMER HAT
Women all over the world know what a new spring hat means. Baa-lamb is no exception, he gets his golden hat through a lot of adventures.

CANDY
Three animals from old Mac Donald's farm are watching when Baa-lamb receives an unexpected birthday gift.

JINGLES
Jingles the clown brags that he is the best clown in the world.'

Figure 102 - Baa-lamb with farm animals   *Figure 103 - Jingles the clown*

Joy was quoted:

"I, for my part, felt it was a great honour to take part in such an important International gathering, which, I'm sure will have far reaching effects on world puppetry. I return home with a renewed faith in my chosen profession – stimulated by seeing so many masterly performances and determined to go forward and produce something which, in its own way will worthily represent at least one aspect of the most complex of all the Arts."

Figure 104 - Joy outside the theatre in Bucharest

As one of the more well-known puppeteers, this trip was an opportunity for Joy to meet others in her field. Some in attendance were:

- *Serghei Obraztzov – Director of the Moscow Central Puppet Theatre.*
- *Dr. Jan Malik – Czechoslovak Republic*
- *Marjorie Batchelder – USA*
- *Ann Hogarth – Great Britain (winning 2nd prize for Interpretation)*
- *Jan Bussell – Great Britain*

The journey to Romania from Great Britain was made by train, where Joy travelled with the Hogarths (Ann, Jan and crew) for company.

Joy took many photographs of Romania on her Delmonta camera during her stay there, and these were not limited to the exhibiting puppets and puppeteers. She was clearly fascinated with the people from the surrounding area, leading a lifestyle that no doubt seemed vastly different to her own life at home in Tiptree. Cataloguing her time there in a methodically organised album, it shows Joy's keen interest in photography in an almost documentary style, making excellent use of the dozen rolls of film she took with her. From photographs of locals laughing in the street to transport ticket stubs, pressed local flowers and ferns, postcards from the show and even her original Customs

Declaration from Victoria Station, London – it is a true time capsule, all annotated with wit.

Figure 105 - The Hogarths in Vienna

Figure 106 - Gigurtu the interpreter

Figure 107 - Mehr Contractor (India), Marjorie Batchelder and Romain Proctor (USA), with two Romanian guides and a driver, in Senia

Figure 108 - Serghei Obraztzov (USSR) playing hopscotch

Figure 109 - The great Dr Jan Malik (Czech Republic)

Figure 110 - Spring onion seller, Bucharest market

Figure 111 - A mother and daughter

Figure 112 - Toy sellers

Figure 113 - Gypsy flower sellers; Joy kept the flowers she bought and pressed them in her album beside this photo

Figure 114 - The "Dance of the Horsemen"

Figure 115 - A curb side joke

Figure 116 - A cart park!

Figure 117 - Romanian rod puppets

Figure 118 - Romanian rod puppets

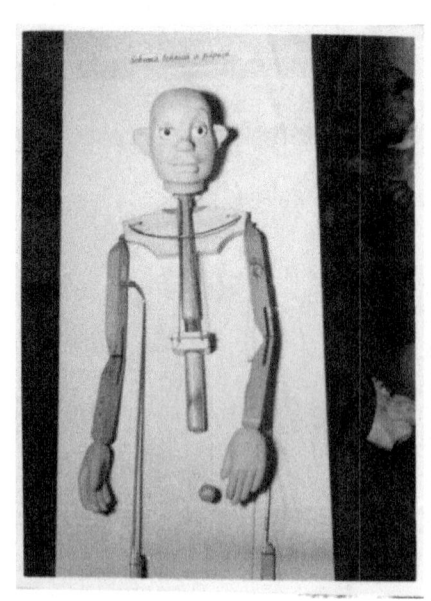

Figure 119 - Russian rod puppet  *Figure 120 - Les Marottes Paris*

Upon her return to Britain, Joy gave a lecture titled 'Working and Playing with Puppets'. It had sections devoted to educational, therapeutic, and practical applications of puppetry. Later in life, Joy would turn once again to these applications of her favourite art form in her work with vulnerable adults.

Just returned from Rumania . . . .

JOY LAUREY

presents her lecture

"Working and Playing with Puppets"

Although descended from a famous theatrical family, Joy Laurey enjoys a considerable prestige in her own right for her work in all fields of Puppetry.

Perhaps best known to audiences in this country as the creator of the famous puppet character "Mr. Turnip" (B.B.C.T.V.) she by no means confines her activities to Films and T.V. but has travelled over 100,000 miles with her Puppets.

Her lecture has been specially designed to cover as many aspects of the subject as possible in the time allotted, but special sections devoted to the Educational, Therapeutic or Practical applications of Puppetry can be included on request.

Cullingford & Co., Ltd., Colchester.

Figure 121 - The flyer for Joy's lecture "Working and Playing with Puppets"

CHAPTER 11 – PAUL AND PETA PAGE

Following their return home after the second world war, the sisters having worked together for ENSA, Joy was happy to continue working in the UK as her reputation as a skilled maker and operator of puppets began to grow. Honor, on the other hand, took a brief respite before deciding she wanted to continue travelling, and so in 1950, her and her fiancé, Ian Robertson, decided to move abroad. Once married, they would be known by the stage names of Paul and Peta Page. Their travelling show specialised in marionettes and they were especially adept at operating multiple puppets simultaneously – a skill they became well known for.

Figure 121 - Ian Robertson and Honor Laurey, also known as Paul and Peta Page

During a sixteen-week tour of Australia in 1951, Ian wrote a letter to *The Stage* thanking the publication for a recent mention of their act in an article. In the letter he mentions that the act is proving a great hit!'

A talented couple, Peta (Honor) was the creative force behind the characters, making the puppets from scratch. Paul (Ian) was a skilled puppeteer and they worked seamlessly together.

Although Paul and Peta started their act in Australia in 1950, they later became regular entertainers in UK theatres during the 1960s and 1970s. Some of their original characters included a trio of cat musicians called Marmalade, Tim and Tom, Jack the Sailor, and a husband-seeking

Duchess. They even had The Hot Dogs: a band of old English sheep dogs that could sing, dance and, often surprisingly, managed to play the odd instrument!

Figure 122 - An advert for Paul and Peta Page's show

During their time back on home soil, the duo spent a summer in Eastbourne with the cast of *The Black and White Minstrel Show*, performed two shows with Danny La Rue and worked with others such as Dick Emery, Tommy Cooper and Ronnie Corbett. They were also in pantomime with John Inman in Birmingham.

Throughout their careers Paul and Peta travelled far and wide to perform their highly respected marionette show. The pair played a season at the famous Hansa Theatre in Hamburg, travelled to America to appear on *The Ed Sullivan Show* in 1958 and a particular highlight was a variety show appearance on both East German TV and the BBC.

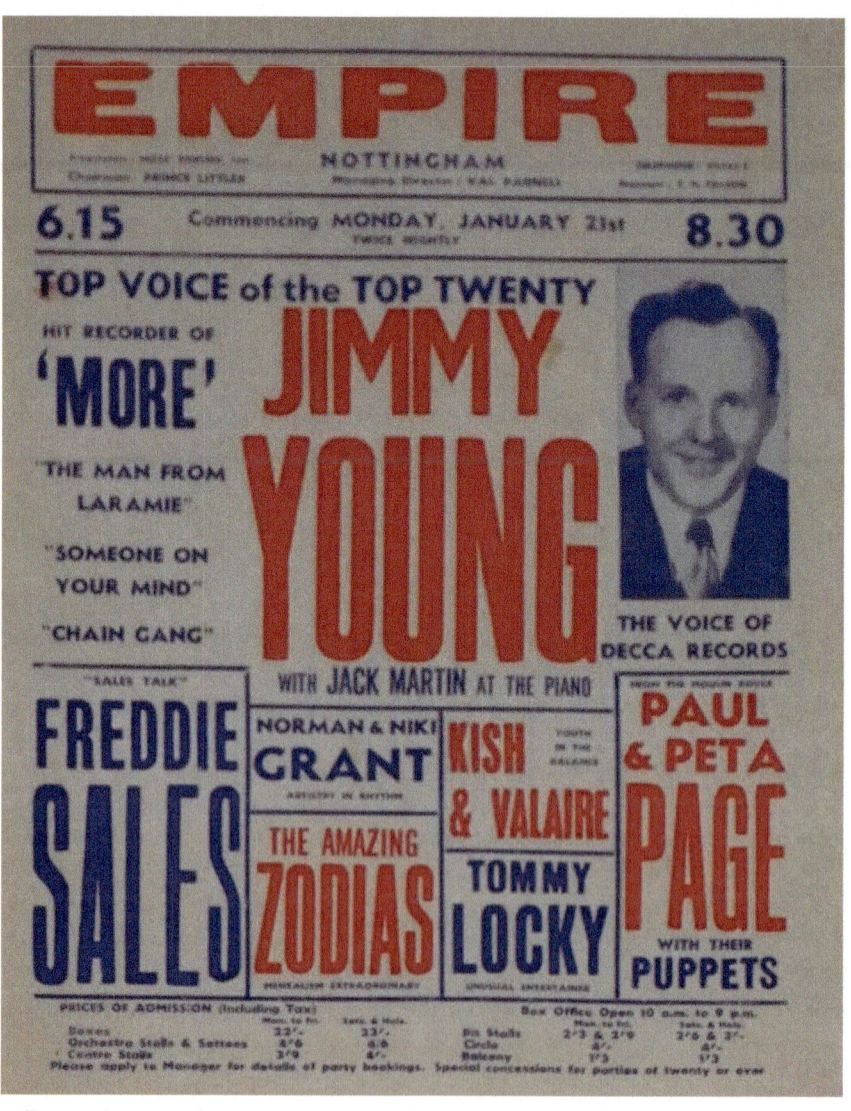

Figure 123 - An advert for Paul and Peta Page can be seen in the bottom right corner of this poster for the 'Empire' theatre

CHAPTER 12 - RETIREMENT & LEGACY

In 1959, The Laurey Puppet Company along with the whole puppetry world sadly lost the valued founding member Dorrie, who died aged 60. The next year Joy married Wladyslaw Luczyc-Wyhowski, a Polish count, lawyer, naval officer and interpreter aboard the Queen Mary and Queen Elizabeth. They raised their two children at home in The Puppet Studio, Tiptree.

Figure 124 - The Puppet Studio as it stands today

Having devoted her career to her passion for puppets, Joy finally hung up the strings to concentrate on her family. Never one to idle, she began working in the Occupational Therapy Department at Severalls Psychiatric Hospital in Colchester. Here she used her creative arts and craft knowledge to help the resident patients. Through music, puppetry, poetry and painting, Joy once again proved her skill and passion could bring happiness and escapism, even in the most unlikely of places. No doubt her old pal Mr Turnip would have accompanied her on a visit or two.

Later she helped open and became the manager of the Woodlands Centre for Disabled People in Colchester.

Home to Joy, her mother Dorrie and sister Honor, and later her husband and children, The Puppet Studio in Tiptree wasn't just their family residence but an active workshop, and even had a small performance hall. Tiptree was the base of operations, ideally situated with the railway station very close by. Joy was able to travel from here to a variety of locations to perform, including her successful summer seasons in Broadstairs, Kent. Still standing today and lovingly maintained, part of the house is thought to be 400 years old. In her interview with Elaine Bamford, author of *Tiptree – Still A Village?*, Joy referenced the unique but likely unwanted feature of bomb shrapnel stuck in the roof! Once known as The Black Horse Beer House, later as a place of worship and then a night school, it now serves as a family home with a historic and colourful past.

Joy crafted many puppets in Tiptree. Looking at the dates she resided there (1949 – 1985) Mr Turnip is but one of them, alongside all the puppets for Gerry Anderson's show *Twizzle*.

Joy once performed in the Tiptree jam factory at the Factory Hall. She performed there alongside other well-known performers such as Peter Brough (a famous TV and Radio star) and his famous ventriloquist puppet Archie Andrews.

In 1985, Joy moved from Tiptree which unfortunately resulted in many years of puppetry memorabilia and even some of the puppets themselves being sold or skipped! The remaining collection, including of course Mr Turnip and a few treasured favourites, thankfully moved with her.

A local family-run company were hired to organise the removal and recycling of Joy's waste. Sorting through the lot, they decided that the boxes and trunks were worth keeping, and they sat neglected in a barn until being found once again in 2020. The following year the find was split into lots and went to auction at a well-known auction house in

Derby. Many of the puppets are badly worn and damaged but this remains an amazing barn-find. This whole collection can now be found in The Joy Laurey Archive.

Figure 125 - A poster for one of the many puppet-related events Joy hosted in Tiptree

In 1991 the University of Essex put on an exhibition in Colchester called *More Than Strings*.

Joy was interviewed at the exhibition about her thoughts on puppetry, the following are excerpts from her responses:

> "Television puppetry is another means of conveying an image and remains an integral part of the development of puppetry in general […] Puppetry has been with us for many years and will continue to be for years to come,

during which, new methods will no doubt be found to convey puppets on television or by any other means."

Regarding the future of puppetry following the introduction of complex animatronics:

> *"...the degree of sophistication and technological wizardry can have little to do with the impact of the final result. The simplest forms of puppetry can sometimes be the most successful."*

It begs the question of what Joy would have thought of the emergence of CGI (computer generated imagery) in film and TV. Recently the film and TV industry has made a return to traditional puppetry, using actual puppets and animatronics, to provide a reference for scale and movement when animating and rendering a 3D model from scratch.

TV series like *The Dark Crystal: Age of Resistance* have proved that the use of puppetry in media remains popular among modern audiences. Director Louis Leterrier confirmed at the 2018 New York Comic Con that the series would rely on puppetry instead of computer animation, only turning to CGI sparingly in the removal of the puppeteers onscreen.

Much like the revival of vinyl records to a modern generation bored with cold digital purity, a respect for the craft of puppetry is bringing the same generation something new and tactile but familiar to their screens. Perhaps even more important to them is its variation from the norm, which can only be seen as a positive movement towards keeping the tradition of puppeteering alive.

I'm sure that Joy, being both talented and straight-talking would have given much practical advice to the way puppetry is used today.

Ted Coney, life-long fan of Mr Turnip, originally met Joy and Mr Turnip when he was a child. Seeing her perform on stage in Scarborough, Ted recalled how glamorous Joy was. He met her again while she was demonstrating the Pelham Puppet version of Mr Turnip at a department store, also in Scarborough, to which Coney was the only person to attend.

A recognised artist and the Head of Art and Design at a Cambridge Sixth Form College, Coney wanted to use the image of his favourite puppet character for a painting representing his childhood.

He decided to track down who currently owned the Mr Turnip puppet and found he was still with his creator Joy. Coney vividly remembers the first telephone conversation he had with Joy: "she had a very young voice, you would have thought she was a young woman in her 20s"

Figure 126 - Joy manipulating Mr Turnip in Ted's home

Joy invited Coney to lunch where she was very welcoming and accommodating. The famous Mr Turnip was always kept safely in a bag and stored inside an old hard tennis case. Joy kindly allowed Coney to make drawings and take photographs of her puppet to use for his painting.

Captivated, he fondly remembers seeing his childhood hero being manipulated by Joy:

> "She moved him so beautifully, it was a power she had in her hands. Joy said she could just "feel it"."

The pair met many more times over the years and a real friendship formed. Joy would visit and entertain Coney's young children with their own private Mr Turnip shows, and she also unveiled his painting titled 'Diamonds'. This painting, featuring 's rendering of his favourite puppet is based on his parents leaving the family home after sixty years. Mr Turnip represents Coney and was painted having a last look around rooms within his childhood home. Coney always had the feeling of being a child when at that house which he felt could never be replicated elsewhere.

When Coney showed Joy some of his working paintings she said, "why are you doing him in colour when you only ever saw him in black and white?". Joy's feedback gave him the inspiration to alternate the background and Mr Turnip in either colour or black and white.

Figure 127 - Ted Coney's painting 'Diamonds'

I met Ted Coney recently when conducting research for this book, and he had such fond memories of the time he spent with Joy and Mr Turnip. Listening to him recall his experiences so vividly and with such passion is a testament to the significance Joy and her vegetable pal had on his life and indeed on the lives of anyone that had the honour of meeting them. Over the years, they exchanged many letters and cards with Joy often sending clips of her own performing past, all of which have been invaluable to me and this book.

I am the proud owner of Mimi Melon, another of Joy's creations who was seen with Mr Turnip on *Whirligig*, and I took her with me to meet Coney at his home and gallery in Ely, Cambridge, where you can see his work on display. He remembers Mimi on TV performing in an Opera sketch whilst Mr Turnip played the piano and remarked that the camera panned up from Mimi to Joy manipulating her, which was very rare for the show.

Joy also gave Coney a copy of her interview on 'Pebble Mill – Puppet Special' from 1983, which featured many well-known puppets, puppeteers, voiceover actors and presenters. It was in fact the first time Joy and HL had seen each other in over thirty years.

In the interview, HL discussed his time on *Whirligig*:

> *"My role was to be the children and have fun, I was always covered in muck[...] Mr Turnip, although twenty-two inches high, was a very strict disciplinarian, he kept me in tow."*

Watching the interview now, it is strange to view as HL had aged yet Mr Turnip did not look any different. Sadly, Humphrey Lestocq died shortly after filming, but it's nice to think these two old friends had one last reunion.

Clive Hicks-Jenkins was another huge fan of Joy and Mr Turnip. He was very lucky to meet the lady herself in 1997, and the following excerpt is from Hicks-Jenkins's own blog recollecting the day.

Figure 127 - Joy with Clive Hicks-Jenkins

'Joy couldn't have been more generous in sharing her memories of her life as a puppet-maker/puppeteer, which were still vivid and fresh. She'd pretty much set aside her puppets after marriage and children, and we spent the afternoon together sifting through old suitcases of memorabilia.

Figure 129 - Joy unveiling Mr Turnip for Hicks-Jenkins

'She told me there were many more puppets stored in boxes her garage (sic), and she rather dreaded the task of going through them all, though she said it with a twinkle, and I could see that in fact she rather relished the idea of time spent examining her past. Had I lived closer I would have volunteered to help.

Figure 130 - Hicks-Jenkins puppeteering Mr Turnip

I walked away from the day with a treasure: a tiny calling-card, almost the last of a small cache Joy had preserved from Mr Turnip's glory days, when children visiting him at the BBC Lime Grove studios would each be presented with a memento from their hero's waistcoat pocket. I keep it in *the marionette cabinet with my own Pelham Puppet Mr Turnip. It's no bigger than a postage stamp, though freighted with memories that make me almost dizzy with happiness.'*

Figure 131 - Even in retirement, Joy remained "the girl that pulls the strings"

Figure 132 - Joy's original Mr Turnip with a Pelham puppet Mr Turnip gifted by Hicks-Jenkins

Joy was interviewed in 1997 by *See Hear Magazine!*, a magazine for the hard of hearing. Joy herself grew deaf in her later years.

Figure 133 - Joy and Mr Turnip on the cover of See Hear Magazine!

She made the front cover alongside Mr Turnip and the article focused not just on her adjusting to deafness, but her lifelong career in puppetry and her love for Mr Turnip.

Joy eventually felt it was time to let Mr Turnip go and live with a new owner who could treasure and enjoy their time with him. He has since been sold multiple times, along with lots of Joy's collected memorabilia.

Figure 134 - Mr Turnip ready for auction (2007)

Vectis Auctions sold Mr Turnip in a 2007 auction for the sum of £3000, complete with his change of clothes and some accessories. Vectis would again handle the bulk of the Joy Laurey collection in a 2020 auction which saw Mr Turnip increase in value.

Figure 135 - Mr Turnip ready for his second auction (2020)

I was lucky enough to acquire a large part of the collection and memorabilia, including many sketches, original watercolours, working documents, photographs, press clippings and personal keepsakes to name but a small selection, which I treasure and without it wouldn't have had the resources for this book. Joy was an avid collector of all things 'Laurey' and thanks to her methodical archiving, I have the material to also publish a website, where I intend to preserve more of her work for everyone to appreciate.

Figure 136 - Some of the auction lots obtained and preserved in The Joy Laurey Archive

Joy was moved to a care home where she sadly passed away on June 2nd 2014, at the grand age of 90, having lived years of fun and adventure which she shared with so many. In her will, she managed one last show of love and generosity to children, leaving a donation to the Barnardo's charity.

Setting a standard for TV puppetry, Joy's work has helped to encourage and entertain children for years. I can't think of a decade that hasn't been dominated by a hit show for children featuring puppets. For me it was the 1980s, with Roland Rat, Basil Brush, Gordon the Gopher to name but a few, not forgetting the great Ronnie Le Drew performing with Zippy on *Rainbow*.

Figure 137 - Ronnie Le Drew and Zippy from 'Rainbow'

I feel extremely passionate about the work Joy did in her lifetime. I believe Joy's legacy will go on, now proudly in this book. No longer confined to auction houses and barns but in the public domain to celebrate and enjoy for many future generations to come.

Figure 138 - The final photo and the one that features on the cover, shows a very happy Joy and her ever loving, admiring vegetable, Mr Turnip

PICTURE CREDITS

I'd like to thank the following for their help and support in making such a comprehensive record of Joy's life. The following are the owners of some of the images in this book, listed according to the figure number subtitling each image.

26. Ted Coney
30. The British Puppet and Model Theatre Group
95. Anderson Entertainment
96. Anderson Entertainment
97. Vectis Auctions Ltd.
101. Vectis Auctions Ltd.
102. Vectis Auctions Ltd.
124. Janet and Tony Chandler
126. Ted Coney
127. Ted Coney
128. Peter Wakelin
129. Peter Wakelin
130. Peter Wakelin
131. Peter Wakelin
132. Peter Wakelin
133. Ted Coney
134. Vectis Auctions Ltd.
135. Vectis Auctions Ltd.
137. Ronnie Le Drew

Other images used that are not credited above fall under the public domain or are royalty free.

SPECIAL THANKS

I'd like to dedicate a special thank you to the following people who have given me so much support in the making of this book and have been incredibly helpful.

Wonky Woman for her generous donation.

Clive Hicks-Jenkins for the use of his blog and photos.

Ian Stewart for assisting with information and research.

Peter Beaven for assisting with information and research.

Ted Coney for sharing his memories and knowledge.

Felice Monk for her discovery of the lost puppets.

Elaine Bamford for the use of interview material.

Tony Chandler for his help with the puppet studio in Tiptree.

The British Puppetry and Model Theatre Guild for the use of their archived material and ongoing support.

Henley Scan for their help digitising the archive material.

And a huge thanks to Matthew Gee – without his help and support, and initial proofing corrections this book wouldn't exist!

I would also like to thank the following people who donated to the crowdfunding page that made this book possible.

Matthew Gee	Felice Monk
Janine Woodhead	Pam and Bob Gee
Ronnie Le Drew	Ted Coney
Lars Peter Beaven	Sian Oxton
Ken Sequin	Timothy Bates
Ian Stewart	Ann Perrin
James Arnott	Tina Underwood
Jamie Ward	Trevor Sprotson
Alison and James McCulley	Rhys Cook
Brand Braithwaite	Dan Lowther

Katy Gaughan
Sam Kelly
Richard Cawkwell
Marie Clements
Brett Jensen
Noella Burns

Jayne Burns
Lewis Marshall
Charlie Trimmings
Sarah Roberts
AndrewWitts

Printed in Great Britain
by Amazon